BREAKING THE SILENCE

A MOTHER'S JOURNEY THROUGH LOSS AND ADVOCACY

TONYA JONES

Library of Congress Control Number: 2025926136

ISBN: 978-1-966612-93-3

Cover Design: Olaniyan Bukola

First Printed Edition: January 2026

Printed in the United States of America

Table of Contents

DEDICATION

"Come to me, all you who are weary and burdened, and I will give you rest." Matthew 11:28

ACKNOWLEDGMENTS

As I write these words, I am filled with profound gratitude for the journey that led me to create Breaking the Silence. This book is not merely a reflection of my grief and healing; it is a tribute to my son, Deterrious Jerome Hayes Jones (DJ), whose life and spirit continue to inspire me every day.

I extend my heartfelt thanks to my family, who have stood by me through the darkest moments of my life. Your unwavering support and love have been my guiding light, reminding me that I am not alone on this journey. To my grandson, Terrion, you are a beacon of hope and joy, and it is for you that I strive to keep DJ's memory alive.

I also want to express my deepest gratitude to the Out of the Darkness Walk. Participating in this event has been life-saving, offering me a sense of community and purpose when my grief felt overwhelming. The shared stories of resilience and the camaraderie have shown me the power of unity in the face of profound loss.

To the friends, family members, and individuals I have met along this journey, thank you for sharing your stories of loss, love, and resilience. Your courage in facing grief has inspired me to be open about my own experiences, and together we have built a community grounded in compassion and understanding.

I am especially grateful to the mental health advocates and organizations dedicated to raising awareness about suicide prevention. Your tireless work shines a light on a topic that too often remains in the shadows, and I am honored to lend my voice to this vital cause.

I give honor, praise, and glory to God for giving me the strength to undertake this journey through tears and pain. Through faith, I find hope, and all praise and glory belong to God.

To all the readers who pick up this book, thank you for joining me on this journey. My hope is that by sharing DJ's story, we can break the silence surrounding mental health and suicide, fostering a culture of openness and support. Let us remember that behind every statistic is a life that mattered, and that together, we can create a world where love and understanding triumph over stigma and silence.

In loving memory of my son, Deterrious Jerome Hayes Jones (DJ), who will forever be in my heart. Mama loves you.

PROLOGUE

I never imagined my life could change so drastically in a single moment. The day I lost my son, DJ, my world shattered. The pain that followed wasn't just emotional; it was physical, like my heart had been ripped from my chest, leaving a hollow space where my joy used to be. I remember screaming, but no sound came out. I remember gasping for air, as if grief had stolen my ability to breathe. I remember the weight of the truth pressing down on me, crushing me under the unbearable reality that he was gone.

I lost more than my child that day. I lost the laughter that once filled our home, the warmth of his presence, the late-night talks where we shared our dreams, and the unspoken bond between a mother and her son. I lost a future that should have been his—a future where he thrived, chased his dreams, and grew into the man I always knew he could be.

DJ wasn't just my son; he was my heart walking outside my body. He had a way of lighting up a room, making people feel like they belonged, and carrying his struggles while lifting others up. His smile—oh, that smile could even fool me. I look back now and wonder how many times I missed the signs. How many times had he been hurting while I thought he was okay?

In that single, irreversible moment, I lost a piece of myself. But in the depths of my pain, something else was born: a mission I never asked for but can no longer ignore. It is a mission forged from the rawness of grief and the unbearable weight of unanswered questions. It is the need to tell DJ's story, to break the silence that too often surrounds mental health, and to ensure that his life, though cut short, continues to make a difference.

This book is more than a tribute to my son. It is my way of making sense of the unimaginable, of searching for meaning in a loss that feels impossible to comprehend. It is my way of reaching out to others who may be suffering in silence, hoping that even one person reading these words finds the strength to seek help—to hold on just a little longer. It is a call to action, a plea for compassion, and a reminder that behind every smile, there may be struggles we cannot see.

I think back to the nights I held DJ in my arms as a baby, rocking him to sleep, whispering promises that I would always protect him. I believed that with everything in me. I was his mother. I was a nurse. I was a caregiver by nature. And yet, I couldn't save him. The guilt of that truth is something I carry every day, though I have learned that guilt is not love. Love is what I choose now: speaking his name, sharing his story, and making sure no other mother feels the way I do.

Writing these pages has been a journey through love and loss, through moments of crippling grief and small glimmers of healing. It has been a way of holding onto DJ, keeping his spirit alive the only way I know how. And as I share this story, I do so with the hope that it will bring comfort, awareness, and perhaps even change.

As you turn these pages, I invite you to walk this journey with me, not just through the heartbreak of loss but also through the enduring light of DJ's legacy. His legacy is one of love, resilience, and hope—a light I carry every single day. I pray that by sharing his story, that light reaches someone who needs it

INTRODUCTION

This is the book I never thought I would write. It is born out of the unimaginable, a loss that no parent, no family, and no community should ever have to endure. My son, DJ, full of light, laughter, and promise, died by suicide. He was 28 years old, and his absence has left an ache in my heart that will never fully heal.

I remember his smile. The kind that could melt any tension, and the way he reached out to others with an openness that was both rare and profound. His laughter could fill a room, and his dreams felt so big they could change the world. His love for his son, his family, and his friends was boundless, reflecting the remarkable person he was. His passing was a shock, leaving not only a grieving family but also unanswered questions and an undeniable truth: silence around suicide can be deadly.

Suicide is a topic that touches far more people than we often admit. Whether through personal struggles or the loss of someone we love, nearly everyone has been impacted by this devastating reality. Yet, despite its prevalence, we still struggle as a society to talk about it openly and without judgment.

This book is my attempt to change that. By sharing my story, I hope to illuminate the ripple effects of suicide, the challenges of navigating loss, and the urgent need for awareness, understanding, and action. It is a story of heartbreak, yes, but also of resilience, love, and hope. Writing it has been one of the hardest things I've ever done, but it is my way of ensuring my son's life and legacy continue to make an impact.

DJ's story is not just about loss; it is about the love and connection he brought into the world. It is about the people he touched and the light he shared, even while carrying burdens he never fully revealed.

To those who have lost someone to suicide, I see you, and I grieve with you. To those struggling with thoughts of suicide, I urge you to hold on. You are not alone, and help is available. And to everyone else, I hope this book equips you with the understanding and tools to be a source of support and compassion for those who need it most.

Together, we can break the silence. Together, we can make a difference.

CHAPTER 1
A Light in the Darkness

When I think of my son, DJ, the first thing that comes to mind is his laughter. Full, unrestrained, and completely contagious. It was the kind of laughter that could brighten even the heaviest day, echoing through hallways and filling entire rooms with warmth. He had a presence that made people feel comfortable, seen, and valued. Whether he was singing a made-up tune, dancing to a rhythm only he seemed to hear, or cracking jokes that left everyone laughing, his joy had a way of pulling everyone into it.

DJ had an innate gift for transformation; he could turn strangers into friends with a single conversation, building connections that felt instant and meaningful. From a young age, he showed a natural ability to understand others. He had a quiet awareness of people's emotions, and he would often go out of his way to ease their stress. I remember countless moments when he noticed a friend feeling low and made it his mission to lift their mood. Whether it was a silly dance, a sincere compliment, or simply listening, DJ had a rare ability to raise people's spirits. Kindness wasn't something he did—it was part of who he was.

After his passing, I was overwhelmed by how many people came forward to share their stories about how my son had helped them. Friends, acquaintances, and even people I had never met described the deep impact he had during their darkest moments. Some shared how he reached out when they felt completely alone, offering hope, encouragement, and kindness when they needed it most. Hearing those stories gave me a small measure of comfort in the middle of the grief, but it also sharpened the painful irony of his own hidden struggles. Realizing that the same person who brought so much light to others was fighting his own shadows left me with a question I still struggle with: how could someone who lifted so many people have been carrying so much darkness himself?

DJ was a man of contradictions. He was always smiling on the outside yet carrying a heaviness he rarely shared. His laughter and joy masked feelings that most people never saw. He loved life, or at least that's what he showed the world. He was the life of the party—the one who would break into a song or lead a dance, his energy pulling everyone in. Watching him, it was hard to believe he could have been struggling with anything internally. It was as if he wore a mask that hid the turmoil underneath.

Family meant everything to DJ, and he especially adored his two-year-old son, who was the center of his world. I was blessed to watch my son grow from a playful child into a loving father. He embraced fatherhood with an open heart, pouring his love and focus into nurturing his son. Their bond was full of laughter, small adventures, and moments that would make any parent proud. DJ was a devoted father, always eager to create memories, whether building pillow forts, playing imaginary games, or reading bedtime stories with a warmth that showed how deeply he cared.

If there was one role DJ cherished above all others, it was being a father. The day his son, Terrion, was born was one of the greatest days of his life. From the moment he held his baby boy, he knew this would be the most important thing he ever did. DJ often said Terrion gave him new life—a fresh sense of purpose. He even gave him a special nickname: Senzu. Inspired by the senzu bean from Dragon Ball Z, which revived or healed characters, DJ saw his son as his own source of renewal. "He's my senzu bean," he would say with a grin. "He gave me that new energy."

He loved being a dad in every way. He sang to Terrion, cuddled him, and proudly showed him off to anyone who would listen. He had big dreams for his son. Dreams of teaching him how to throw a football, how to ride a bike, and how to be strong, kind, and fearless. Even though their time together was short, DJ poured all the love he had into his son. In many ways, Terrion carries his father's spirit forward: a living extension of DJ's love and legacy.

As I look back on those moments, I see how deeply DJ's love for his son was connected to the struggles he carried. Becoming a father gave him a renewed sense of purpose and joy, but it also brought pressure—

expectations he felt responsible for meeting. The weight of being a provider, a role model, and a steady presence often felt overwhelming. When I sit with these memories, I find myself facing the full complexity of his life: the happiness he created with his son and the quiet battles he fought within himself.

In the days leading up to May 4, 2023, I sensed a heaviness in him that I had never seen before. DJ had always been committed to his job at a home health agency in De Soto, Texas, working long hours to take care of his family. But something was different. His employer refused to pay him the overtime he had rightfully earned, and even after multiple attempts to address the issue, he was dismissed and ignored. The pressure of financial uncertainty, paired with his determination to provide for his son, weighed on him in a way that was impossible to overlook. The stress was unlike anything I had ever witnessed in him.

As the days unfolded in early May 2023, I could sense a heaviness in my son that I had never seen before. He had always been a hardworking man, passionately dedicated to his job with a home health agency in De Soto, Texas. His commitment to caring for his patients was unwavering, often going above and beyond to ensure their needs were met. But in those last days, the weight of his responsibilities began to crush him.

The issues with his employer had escalated to a breaking point. Despite working countless hours, often covering for other staff members, he faced a distressing reality: the agency refused to pay him for the overtime he had worked. He had approached the owner multiple times, seeking resolution through conversations and text messages, but each attempt was met with denial and excuses. Rather than addressing the situation or acknowledging his hard work, the owner seemed more focused on destroying my son's name, spreading false narratives that undermined his integrity. The frustration was palpable, and I could see it etched on his face, the worry growing deeper with each passing moment.

Between May 1 and May 3, he complied with every request from the agency, providing documentation and evidence of the hours he had worked, all in hopes of securing the payment he desperately needed to support himself and his son. As a father, the weight of financial uncertainty bore down on him, and I could see how much he wanted to be there for his child, to provide the stability that every parent dreams of.

But it wasn't just the financial strain that troubled him. As the tension mounted, he began receiving threatening messages from the owner of the agency, words that cut deep and added to his already fragile state of mind. He shared these texts with me, and I could feel the anguish in his voice as he spoke about the situation. I understood that his mental health struggles complicated everything, amplifying his fears and feelings of inadequacy.

While I don't believe that these circumstances alone were the cause of my son's decision, I recognized them as the final straw, the relentless pressure that had been building for far too long. I felt helpless, watching him carry a burden that seemed insurmountable, and I wished with all my heart that I could take that pain away.

On the evening of May 3, 2023, my son came to visit me. He sat with me for hours that night, and we laughed and talked like we always did. It was one of those simple, beautiful moments that I now treasure more than anything. He spent the rest of the evening with his cousin, who was more like a little brother to him. They caught up on life, joked around, and enjoyed each other's company like brothers do.

He spent the night of May 3 with me, and we talked and laughed like we always did. I didn't know it would be the last time I saw my son alive. The next morning, he sent me a text: "Momma, I love you."

I replied immediately, "Baby, I love you too." I never could have imagined those would be our final words. Later that day, when I received the phone call, my heart sank. The world around me blurred, and time slowed to an agonizing crawl. I gripped the steering wheel as I rushed to his house, my mind racing with desperate thoughts, holding on to the hope that there had been some kind of mistake. That maybe, just maybe, things weren't as bad as they seemed. But as the minutes ticked by and the drive to my son's house stretched on, I could feel that hope slipping away, piece by piece.

I was on the freeway, and it felt like time had slowed to a crawl. Every mile felt endless, every second more excruciating. The car seemed to move slower with each passing minute, my thoughts racing even faster. I replayed the conversation over and over in my head, searching for a clue I might have missed. Something that would tell me this wasn't true. But deep down, I knew the truth. My heart was telling me what my mind didn't want to admit.

I thought about him: the way he always had that smile that could light up a room, the way he would laugh and joke, making everyone around him feel better even if he was hurting. But now, none of that mattered. I couldn't hold onto the images of him the way I wanted to. I had to face what was in front of me. The dread that had been sitting in the pit of my stomach began to grow, and as I approached his street, it felt like the world was suffocating me.

But when I arrived and saw the ambulance pulling away, reality crashed down on me with a force I could barely withstand. The air was heavy with silence, and my heart shattered into a million irreparable pieces. But I couldn't ignore the truth staring me in the face. There was no mistaking it now. I'd been holding onto a thread of hope, a tiny part of me that thought maybe this was all a mistake, but as soon as I saw that ambulance leave, I knew.

I had hoped this was some kind of cruel mistake, but as I stood there, it became all too real. He was gone.

There was no escaping it. No going back to a life before this moment. It was over. My heart shattered as I stepped forward, the weight of my son's absence overwhelming every part of me. How could this be real? How could I have missed the signs? As I stood there, looking at his door, the questions I would carry with me for the rest of my life began to form: What did I miss? Could I have done something?

In that moment, I understood something I'd never known before: Grief isn't just a feeling. It's an all-consuming force that shifts the course of your existence. The days and weeks after DJ's passing were filled with unbearable pain, questions with no answers, and a relentless storm of emotions. I found myself trapped between memories of his laughter and the unshakable sorrow of his absence. Each recollection was both a comfort and a torment, reminding me of what I had lost and what could never be again.

Yet amid the grief, a quiet resolve began to take root. I could not allow my son's story to fade into darkness. DJ's life was a testament to love, resilience, and the profound impact one person can have on the world. I knew, with unwavering certainty, that his legacy needed to live on, not just in memory, but in action.

By sharing his story, I hope to inspire others to find their own light amid darkness, to seek help when they need it, and to reach out to those who may be struggling. My goal is that this journey will not only honor my son's memory but also spark meaningful conversations about mental health, resilience, and the power of love and connection.

DJ may have left this world, but the light he shared continues to shine brightly in the hearts of those he touched.

CHAPTER 2:

Unbreakable Bonds: The Story of DJ and His Family

March 13, 1995, is a date forever etched in my heart. A day that transformed my world in ways I could never have imagined. On that day, my son DJ entered this world, bringing a joy unlike anything I had ever known. He was my first child, my only child, and the moment I laid eyes on him; an overwhelming wave of love swept over me like a warm embrace. DJ was a beautiful baby, with bright eyes that sparkled with curiosity and a smile that could light even the darkest days. He had a full head of soft, dark curls, tiny hands that instinctively wrapped around my fingers, and a presence that immediately filled every space with warmth.

From the moment he was placed in my arms, I knew he was mine, and I was his—a love so fierce, so all-encompassing, it felt as though my heart had expanded in ways I never thought possible.

From the very beginning, our bond was unshakable. I would cradle him for hours, feeling the rhythm of his tiny heartbeat against my chest, his soft breath tickling my skin as he slept. In those early days, life revolved around his every need: feedings, diaper changes, lullabies in the middle of the night. But beyond the routines of new motherhood, there was a deeper connection—something sacred. I would whisper to him as I rocked him in the quiet hours, making promises only a mother could make: I will protect you. I will always be here.

Those early days were filled with wonder. Every milestone—his first smile, his first laugh, the first time his tiny hands reached for my face felt like a miracle. I can still hear his giggles, that infectious baby laugh with the power to erase even the hardest days. When he took his first wobbly steps, I clapped so loudly he startled himself, falling back onto his little bottom before bursting into laughter.

As DJ grew into a toddler, his personality began to blossom. He was full of energy and zest for life, always eager to explore and play. His vivid imagination made every day an adventure. His love for superheroes began early, but Spider-Man was his absolute favorite. He would run around the house, arms outstretched, pretending to shoot webs from his tiny fingers, making swooshing noises as if swinging from the ceiling. Sometimes I would humor him, pretending to be the villain he had to capture. He would laugh so hard when I dramatically fell to the floor, "defeated" by his web-slinging powers.

Even at that age, he wanted to be someone who saved people. He believed in heroes—not just the ones in comic books, but the ones in real life too. "Mommy, I wanna be strong like Spider-Man, but I don't wanna fight people. I just wanna help 'em," he once told me, his big brown eyes filled with innocence and conviction. His playfulness and joy extended to every part of his life.

I can still picture him in his little T-ball uniform. A miniature version of a budding athlete, beaming with pride as he stepped onto the field. With his cap slightly askew and his bat clutched tightly in his small hands, he radiated innocence and joy. Every game was an adventure, and I cherished the moments spent cheering him on from the sidelines, my heart swelling with pride as he swung at the ball, sometimes missing and sometimes connecting with a satisfying crack that echoed across the field.

DJ's laughter was infectious, ringing through the air like a melody. He had a unique ability to make everyone around him smile. Whether through his silly antics or the way he danced with abandon, completely lost in the moment. He was a natural performer, always ready to entertain, whether in our living room or in front of family and friends. His joy was a gift, and I was grateful every day for the light he brought into our lives. Family gatherings were his stage. He had a magnetic personality and a natural charm that made him the center of attention. Not because he sought it, but because he radiated joy. I remember holiday celebrations where he ran around, playing with cousins, his laughter filling the air like music. I often found myself sitting back, watching in awe as he created memories that would last a lifetime.

Family was everything to DJ. From the moment he entered this world, he was surrounded by a love so deep and unshakable it became the foundation of his life. His relationships with his grandmother, T.T. Angie, his Uncle Eric, his cousins, and, most importantly, his son shaped him into the young man he became. They weren't just family—they were his safe haven, his biggest cheerleaders, his greatest sources of joy.

He loved his grandmother. Everyone in the family called her "Mother," but to DJ, she was always "Meme." As soon as he started talking, he made that distinction, and from that day forward, the name stuck. She was his heart, and he was hers. Their connection went beyond words, beyond even the bond of grandmother and grandson. It was as if their souls had recognized each other long before he was born.

Meme was there from the beginning, holding him in her arms, rocking him to sleep, whispering prayers over him. She spoiled him in the way only a grandmother could—not just with gifts, but with patience, understanding, and a love so unconditional it felt almost sacred. No matter how big he got, DJ always found comfort in her presence. Even as he grew older, he would curl up beside her, resting his head in her lap while she ran her fingers through his hair, just as she had when he was a little boy. He never liked to see her upset. If she wasn't herself, DJ would do everything in his power to bring a smile to her face. Whether it was a joke, a silly dance, or simply wrapping his arms around her and saying, "I love you, Meme," he always made sure she knew how much she meant to him. And Meme—she adored him in a way words could never fully capture. He was her baby, her pride and joy, and that never changed, not even as he grew into a young man.

If Meme was his heart, T.T. Angie was his anchor. She was more than an aunt; she was a second mother, a protector, a guide through life's ups and downs. From the moment DJ was born, T.T. Angie was there, loving him as if he were her own.

Their relationship was filled with warmth, laughter, and a trust that few people get to experience. She was the one he could turn to for anything, knowing she would always offer honesty wrapped in love. She would tell him when he was wrong, encourage him when he was right, and lift him up when he needed strength.

"Boy, you know I love you," she would always say, shaking her head at one of his antics.

"And I love you more, T.T. Angie," he'd always respond with a grin, knowing full well she'd argue otherwise.

She showed up for him in every way that mattered. Whether at school events, family gatherings, or during everyday life, she was always there—present, attentive. Her love for DJ was unwavering, and in return, he cherished her like a second mother.

As DJ entered elementary school, his love for sports deepened, and he discovered a new passion: flag football.

I can still see him in his colorful jersey, excitement shining in his bright eyes and wide grin as he ran onto the field, ready to tackle the game head-on. He loved the thrill of competition, the camaraderie with his teammates, and the adrenaline rush that came with every play. But what truly stood out was how he would often glance into the stands, searching for his Uncle Eric's approval.

To everyone else, he was Eric, but to DJ, he was always "Unc." From the time he was a little boy, DJ looked up to his uncle as if he hung the moon. If Meme was his heart and T.T. Angie his anchor, Unc was his inspiration. He wanted to be just like him: to carry himself with confidence, make people laugh, and live life with strength and purpose.

Uncle Eric was not just a beloved family member; he was DJ's idol. Their bond was special filled with laughter, stories, and deep mutual respect. DJ would scan the bleachers, his gaze lighting up the moment he spotted Eric. It was as if he drew strength and encouragement from his uncle's presence. Whether he made a great play or fumbled the ball, DJ always sought Eric's nod of approval or a thumbs-up, his face glowing with pride when he received it. That connection served as both motivation and comfort. A reminder that, no matter what the outcome, he had someone in his corner cheering him on.

Their bond was built on more than admiration; it was rooted in the countless memories they made together. Unc taught DJ many lifelong lessons. He was the one DJ could always count on for advice—the one who would listen without judgment, offering wisdom in his own unique way. Whenever DJ played football, his eyes would immediately scan the crowd, searching for Unc. It didn't matter how many people were cheering; his uncle's approval was the only one that truly mattered. DJ thrived on that connection, knowing that whether he scored a touchdown or fumbled the ball, Unc would always be there, nodding in support and making him feel like a champion.

One game stood out. DJ had just made an incredible catch, sprinting down the field with everything he had. As the crowd erupted in cheers, he didn't turn to celebrate with his teammates. Instead, he looked straight to the stands, searching for that familiar face. There was Unc, beaming with pride and throwing his fist in the air in celebration. That was all DJ needed. That was everything. Their relationship wasn't just about sports; it was about guidance, shared wisdom, and knowing that no matter what happened in life, DJ had someone in his corner who believed in him unconditionally.

The bond we shared was more than mother and son; it was a partnership, a friendship that grew as he did. I treasured the quiet moments. Reading bedtime stories or sharing secrets during late-night chats. DJ often curled up next to me, his head resting on my shoulder as we lost ourselves in fantastical tales. I valued those moments, knowing they laid the foundation for a relationship built on love, trust, and understanding.

As DJ grew, he embraced new adventures—trying out for sports teams, joining school clubs, or exploring the world with insatiable curiosity. Every experience was a chance to learn and grow, and I was always there to encourage him, cheer him on, and remind him of the potential within him. He was a child who believed in the magic of life, and I was honored to guide him.

Reflecting on those early years, I realize how profoundly they shaped both DJ and me. Each day was a new chapter, filled with laughter, love, and unforgettable moments. The joy of being his mother was a gift I cherished deeply, and I often marveled at the bond we shared. It was a bond that carried us through countless adventures, trials, and triumphs. A bond that ultimately defined our relationship and shaped the legacy of love DJ would leave behind.

DJ was surrounded by love. He lived knowing he was cherished, supported, and valued beyond measure. The love of Meme, T.T. Angie, Unc, his cousins, and his beloved son gave him a foundation so strong it could never be shaken. Even now, their love hasn't faded. It endures in the stories they tell, the memories they hold close, and the way they carry him with them every day. He may no longer be physically here, but the bonds that shaped him remain strong, real, and alive. Through them, DJ's light continues to shine: his love, his laughter, his beautiful spirit—all lives on in the hearts of those who loved him most.

CHAPTER 3:
The Hardest Goodbye

Nothing in this world could have prepared me for planning my child's funeral. As a mother, you spend your life making choices to ensure your child's happiness, safety, and future. But never, not in my worst nightmares, did I imagine I would have to decide how to lay my son to rest.

DJ had always spoken about returning home to Louisiana. As much as I wished I didn't have to fulfill that wish under these circumstances, I knew I had to honor it. Taking my baby back home was one of the hardest things I have ever done. Something no parent should ever face. The pain was unbearable. And yet, in the midst of my grief, my family stood beside me, holding me up when I felt I might collapse under the weight of it all.

The day of the funeral arrived, and I felt like I was moving through a fog. People came from everywhere. Family, friends, teammates, classmates—each carrying their own grief, their own memories of DJ. The love in the room was overwhelming, yet nothing could ease the emptiness I felt inside.

Speakers shared stories of DJ's kindness, his infectious laughter, and his unwavering love for those around him. I listened, holding onto every word, trying to imprint each story on my heart.

When it was my turn to speak, I wanted so badly to say something, to share my love for DJ with the people who had gathered. But as I stepped forward, I felt weighed down, frozen in place. My body was there, standing at the casket, but my mind felt distant, as if I were trapped in a dream I couldn't wake from. I reached out, rubbing his hand, stroking his cheek, desperate to feel some connection, some warmth. The words I wanted to say never came. Instead, I just stood there—lost in the moment, unable to move, unable to speak, but holding onto him for as long as I could. How do you say goodbye to your baby?

How do you sum up a lifetime of love in just a few minutes? My voice cracked, tears fell, but I spoke to him. I told him how proud I was to be his mother, how much he had changed my life, and how deeply he would be missed but never forgotten. I had a conversation with my son.

As we arrived at the cemetery, the reality of it all became suffocating. DJ's close friends and his cousin, who was more like a brother, carried him to his final resting place with quiet strength. My heart ached watching them, knowing how much they loved him and how much they wished this moment weren't real.

The pastor spoke, his voice steady, offering words of comfort that barely reached my ears. During the service, his son came to my brother and said, "I want to kiss my daddy." Without hesitation, my brother lifted him so he could kiss his daddy one last time. The sight broke me in ways I cannot put into words. A tender yet devastating farewell from a child to his father. I was lost in my own grief, my mind clouded by sorrow. As the ceremony proceeded, I held something in my hands that carried immeasurable meaning: a small, soft blanket that had belonged to his son when he was born. With trembling hands, I placed it inside the casket—a piece of love from his baby boy. It felt like the only gift I could still give him, a reminder that even in his absence, his love as a father would never fade.

As the casket was lowered, I felt my soul breaking. I reached for a single rose, my fingers shaking, and dropped it onto the gleaming surface, whispering through my sobs how much I loved him.

This moment wasn't just devastating for me; it shattered my mother, his Meme, and his son. Seeing their grief was unbearable. Watching Meme hold onto my brother for support, her body trembling with emotion. And little Terrion, too young to fully understand, yet sensing that something was profoundly wrong. My heart broke not only for my loss but for theirs as well.

As I walked away, my legs felt weak, my heart heavy. But my family was there, surrounding me with their love, reminding me that I was not alone. My brother, my family, my friends—they held me up when I couldn't stand on my own. I clung to them, grateful beyond words for their strength, their presence, the way they carried me when I felt like I couldn't take another step. I took my baby home to Louisiana. I fulfilled his wish. And though it broke me, I found solace in knowing he was where he wanted to be.

This was the hardest goodbye. A goodbye no mother should ever have to say. Even in that dark moment, I knew one thing with absolute certainty: DJ's love, his light, and his presence would not fade. He would stay with me. Always.

Losing my son taught me something I never expected: suicide doesn't always look the way we think it does. For years, I believed the common myths that people who are suicidal always seem depressed, that they pull away from others, that the signs are obvious. But DJ showed me how untrue that can be.

He was outgoing, charismatic, and full of life, or at least that's how it looked. He didn't pull away from his family or friends. He didn't stop smiling, singing, or joking. On the surface, he seemed steady, centered, in control. That's why his death shocked everyone who knew him. I went over every moment, again and again, trying to find something I missed. The truth is that mental health struggles don't always match our expectations. A person can be hurting and still appear happy. They can be surrounded by people who love them and still feel alone. They can be the ones lifting everyone else while quietly falling apart inside.

One night, a close friend said, "I never imagined DJ was struggling. He was always the one who made me laugh." That's when it hit me: we often confuse outward joy with real peace.

Awareness matters. We need to challenge the stereotypes surrounding mental health and pay attention to what's beneath the surface. We need spaces where people can speak openly and be met with compassion instead of judgment. Through this process, I've learned to notice the smaller signals—the moments when someone's smile doesn't match their eyes, the times their laughter feels pushed, the situations where they start giving things away or saying goodbye in ways that seem final.

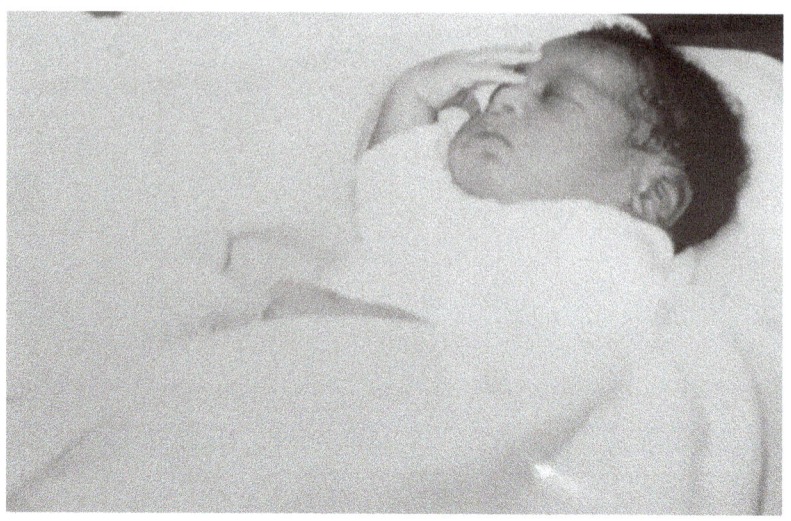

But more importantly, I've learned the impact of asking. Asking, "Are you okay?" Asking, "How are you really doing?" Asking, "Do you need help?" These questions can feel uncomfortable, but they matter. DJ once told me, "Mom, sometimes people just need to know someone cares enough to ask."

If there's one message I want to leave with the world, it's this: don't wait for the signs to be unmistakable. Don't assume someone is fine just because they seem fine. Ask. Reach out. Show up. You never know whose life you might help save.

After losing DJ, I started questioning everything I thought I understood about mental health. How could someone so loved, so full of life, feel so alone? How could someone who brought so much joy to others not feel any for himself? These questions stayed with me, but they also pushed me to learn more. I began studying mental health, suicide prevention, and the factors that feed hopelessness. I went to seminars, talked with professionals, and spent time listening to survivors. What I found was painful but clarifying: mental health struggles don't discriminate. They reach people across every background, at every age, in every community.

These questions haunted me, but they also drove me to learn more. I began researching mental health, suicide prevention, and the factors that contribute to feelings of hopelessness. I attended seminars, spoke with experts, and immersed myself in stories of survivors. What I discovered was heartbreaking but eye-opening: mental health struggles don't discriminate. They affect people from all walks of life, regardless of their age, race, or background.

One of the hardest truths I had to face was that my son didn't take his life because he didn't love us or because he lacked love. He did it because he was in pain, pain so deep and overwhelming he couldn't see another option. Understanding this didn't make the loss easier, but it helped me release some of the guilt. I remember sitting in DJ's room one evening, holding his favorite hoodie, whispering, "I'm sorry I didn't see your pain." It took time for me to understand that even in his silence, he had been asking for help in ways I didn't yet know how to recognize.

Through my journey, I've come to see that education is one of our strongest tools in the fight against suicide. The more we understand about mental health, the better we can support the people who are struggling. We need to talk about it openly and honestly, without shame or stigma. We need to teach our children that it's okay to ask for help and that their feelings matter.

Most of all, we need to listen. Many people reach out in ways that aren't obvious. Sometimes it shows up in their silence. Other times it's in their jokes or in small shifts in their behavior. If we don't slow down enough to truly listen, we risk missing those signals entirely.

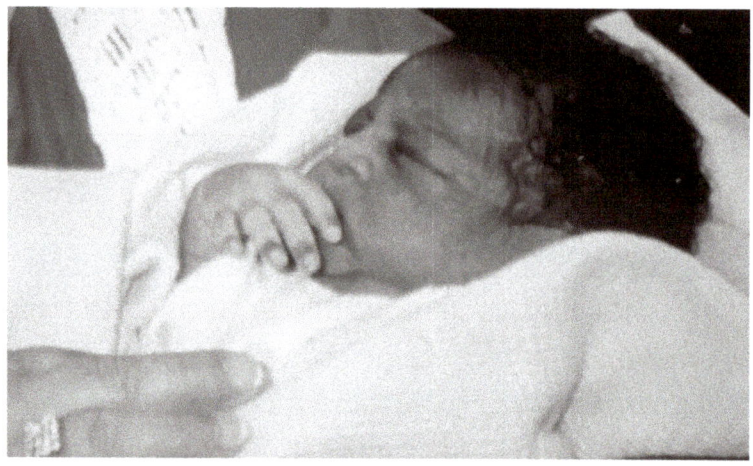

Looking back, I see DJ not as a tragedy, but as a teacher. His story has given me a purpose: to raise awareness, foster understanding, and advocate for change. If sharing his story helps even one person feel less alone, then his light continues to shine.

CHAPTER 4:
Coping with Loss

Grief is a journey I never wanted to take, yet it's a path I've had to learn to face every day since May 4, 2023. Losing my son felt like losing a part of myself. In the first moments after his passing, I was hit with a level of pain that made it hard to breathe. Everything around me seemed to stop, pulling me into a silent space filled only with memories of his laughter and the moments we shared.

For a while, I felt stuck in a dark place, overwhelmed by a sorrow that seemed to pull me under. The weight of my grief was so heavy that imagining any kind of future felt impossible. I questioned everything—why this happened, how I didn't see the signs, and how I was supposed to keep living without him. I replayed pieces of his life, searching for anything I might have missed, hoping that understanding the "why" would ease even a fraction of the pain. There were moments when the loss felt so crushing that I wondered if continuing to live made sense at all. A part of me believed the world might be better without the depth of my suffering.

Yet even during the bleakest hours, small traces of hope started to break through. I was reminded of the love that still surrounded me. My family became my anchor. My mother, brother, and sister-in-law stayed close, steady in their support even when I felt lost. Their presence grounded me, offering strength when I felt emptied out. They sat with me, sometimes in silence, sometimes sharing stories that made me laugh through tears, reminding me I wasn't alone in what I was carrying. My faith was tested in ways I never expected, but I held onto the belief that God had a purpose, even in this pain. In quiet moments of prayer, I searched for calm, hoping for guidance and peace.

I also learned the value of leaning on others for support. Conversations with friends, prayer, and counseling became essential parts of my healing. Grief can be isolating, but it doesn't have to be. There is real strength in letting others carry you when you feel too weak to stand. I found support groups where people shared their experiences of loss, forming a connection that's hard to put into words. Hearing others tell their stories made me feel less like an outcast in my pain and more like part of a community bound by love and loss. The tears, laughter, and shared stories in those spaces became meaningful reminders that we all carry scars.

In exploring grief, I found refuge in creative outlets. Writing became a sanctuary where I could express feelings that were hard to put into words. Journaling, composing letters to DJ, and even writing poems provided a cathartic release. Each word I wrote was a step toward processing my emotions, a way to honor his memory while allowing my heart to heal. Writing felt like a conversation with him—a means of keeping him close even in his absence. I also discovered that grief could be expressed through art, music, and nature. The world around me became a canvas for my sorrow and a space for healing. I found comfort in painting, letting colors flow freely to reflect my emotions—sometimes dark and stormy, other times bright and hopeful.

Throughout this journey, I've found solace in knowing that DJ's love will always be a part of me. Despite my pain, I realized I needed to be strong for his son. Even though I lost my son, he lost his dad. That awareness gave me purpose, motivating me to cope—not just for myself, but for him. I often think about the lessons I want to pass on to my grandson about resilience, love, and the importance of seeking help.

I want him to understand that it's okay to feel pain, but it's equally important to seek joy and connection. I envision a future where I can share stories about his father, keeping DJ's spirit alive while teaching the value of love and mental health awareness.

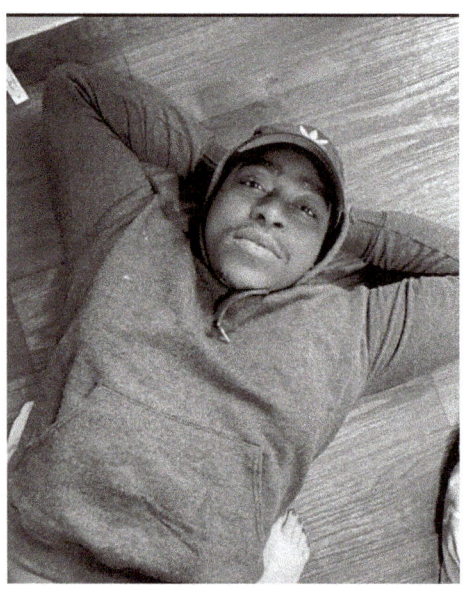

In moments of connection with DJ's memory, I came to understand that grief is not about moving on—it's about moving forward while carrying the love we shared. I've learned that grief reflects the depth of our love. Healing, I now see, is about finding a way to keep living—not by letting go of DJ, but by holding onto him in a way that allows me to embrace life again. This process is not linear; it ebbs and flows, sometimes hitting me with waves of emotion when I least expect them.

Some days, the pain resurfaces, feeling as sharp as it did on that fateful day. Yet there are also moments when I can smile at the thought of him, cherishing the joy he brought to my life and the lives of others. Healing is not a destination—it's a journey of ups and downs, and an acknowledgment that it's okay to embrace both.

There are days when the pain resurfaces, and it feels just as sharp as it did on May 4, 2023. But there are also days when I can smile at the thought of him, remembering the joy he brought to my life and the lives of so many others. Healing is not a destination; it's a journey, filled with ups and downs, moments of joy intertwined with sadness, and the realization that it's okay to embrace both.

As I continue on this path, I carry with me the lessons DJ's life and passing have imparted. They've taught me the importance of compassion, the strength found in vulnerability, and the enduring power of love. I've become more attuned to the struggles of those around me, recognizing that everyone carries their own burdens. This awareness has ignited a passion within me to advocate for mental health, raise awareness about the signs of depression and suicide, and create a dialogue about grief that breaks the silence surrounding it.

I've learned the importance of checking in on friends, asking the hard questions, and being open about my own struggles to encourage others to do the same. Though the pain will always be part of me, so too will the love. That love gives me the strength to keep going. My mission has shifted from merely surviving each day to finding ways to honor DJ's legacy. I've started speaking at community events, sharing my story in the hope that it might resonate with someone who feels lost in their grief.

Though the pain will always be a part of me, so too will the love. And it's that love that gives me the strength to keep going. My mission has transformed from merely surviving each day to finding ways to honor DJ's legacy. I've started to speak at community events, sharing my story in the hopes that it might resonate with someone else who feels lost in their grief. In finding a way to live with my grief, I've discovered that love, even in the face of loss, is the greatest source of healing.

In learning to live with my sorrow, I've discovered that love, even in the face of loss, is the greatest source of healing. By sharing my experience, I hope to show others that they are not alone, that there is a way through the darkness, and that it is possible to find joy again, even when it feels unimaginable. Grief may be a journey, but it can lead to deeper connections, greater empathy, and a renewed appreciation for the value of life.

As I reflect on this journey, I realize that grief has transformed me in ways I never anticipated. It has deepened my understanding of love and loss, teaching me that vulnerability is not a weakness but a strength. I've learned to embrace the complexity of my emotions, allowing myself to feel joy and sorrow simultaneously. This duality has become part of my existence, reminding me that it is okay to laugh while still carrying the weight of my grief.

In quiet moments, I often find myself talking to DJ, sharing my thoughts and feelings as if he were still here. I tell him about my day, my struggles, and my small victories. I share my dreams for the future and the lessons I hope to pass on to his son. These conversations, though one-sided, bring comfort and a sense of connection that transcends physical absence. They remind me that love endures, even when the person we cherish is no longer with us.

As I navigate this path, I recognize the importance of self-care. Grief can be all-consuming, but I've learned that taking time for myself is essential.

Whether it's going for a walk in nature, practicing mindfulness, or simply allowing myself to rest, these moments of self-compassion help me recharge and maintain balance. Nurturing my own well-being enables me to be more present for others, especially my grandson, who needs me now more than ever.

In sharing my story, I hope to inspire others to embrace their grief and find their own paths to healing. This journey requires patience and understanding, both for oneself and for those around us. I want others to know that it's okay to seek help, lean on friends and family, and express emotions openly. Grief is not a solitary experience; it is a shared human condition that connects us all.

As I continue to walk this path, I carry DJ's memory with me, honoring his life by living mine fully. I strive to be a source of light for others navigating their own grief, offering support and understanding. In doing so, I find purpose and meaning in my pain, transforming it into a force for good. Grief may be a journey filled with challenges, but it is also one that can lead to profound growth and connection.

I am learning to embrace the beauty of life, even in the face of loss, and to cherish the moments that remind me of the love that will forever remain in my heart.

CHAPTER 5
Honoring My Son's Legacy

Losing my son has been the most painful experience of my life, but even in my grief, I've found ways to honor his memory and ensure that his legacy continues to shine. For me, this has meant turning my pain into purpose: using my story to bring attention to the importance of mental health and suicide prevention. The journey of honoring my son, DJ, has been both a path of healing and a commitment to ensuring that his life continues to make a difference in the world.

I've also made it a priority to share DJ's story whenever I can. Whether it's through speaking engagements, social media, or simply talking to someone who is struggling, I believe that his story has the power to inspire change. Each time I stand before an audience or engage in conversation, I feel as though I'm keeping his light alive, ensuring that his life continues to make an impact. His life was full of love, laughter, and kindness, and I want the world to remember him for those qualities, not just for how he died. It is a powerful reminder that our loved ones are more than their struggles; they are the sum of their experiences, the joy they brought, and the love they gave.

Honoring his legacy has also meant being there for his son, my grandson. Watching him grow has been both a joy and a challenge. There are moments when I see DJ in him: in the way he smiles, the way he laughs, and even the way he plays, and it brings both comfort and pain. I see glimpses of his father's spirit in those small moments, and it reminds me that DJ's essence endures through his son. But despite the bittersweet moments, I know that my grandson needs me to be present for him, to ensure he grows up surrounded by the same love and support DJ gave to so many.

I tell him stories about his dad: how he had a passion for writing new music and singing with a voice that could move mountains. I remember one time when he was still in elementary school; he sang "We Are the World" with such heartfelt emotion that it brought tears to my eyes. I had no idea how beautiful his voice was until that moment, and it felt like he was sharing a part of himself that was pure and profound. There were also times when he would come to my house with a big smile and say, "Mama, I'm gonna cook for you." And he did just that! It may not have been the way I would have done it: there would be flour on the floor and dishes piled high, but the effort he put into surprising me and my mother made those moments incredibly special. His joy in cooking for us, even if it turned into a delightful mess, was a testament to his love and thoughtfulness. My mother would beam with pride, and I felt so cherished. Sharing these stories with my grandson is so important to me; I want him to know that his dad was not only talented and kind but also someone who brought joy and laughter into our lives through the simplest acts of love.

Honoring DJ's legacy isn't just about remembering him; it's about making sure that his life continues to make a difference. It's about carrying his light forward and using it to guide others out of the darkness. I've found strength in advocating for mental health awareness, sharing resources, and encouraging people to seek help without fear of judgment. Every small act of advocacy feels like a step toward preventing another family from experiencing this same loss. I've organized information sessions in local schools, hoping to equip young people with the tools they need to recognize when they or someone they care about is in distress. It's fulfilling to know that in some small way, I may be contributing to a future where fewer families have to navigate the tragedy of losing a loved one to suicide.

Through this journey, I've connected with other parents who have lost children to suicide. Hearing their stories and sharing my own has been both heartbreaking and healing. It reminds me that while the pain of loss is unique to each of us, we are united by a shared purpose: honoring our children's lives and preventing others from experiencing the same tragedy. These connections have created a support network I never expected to find. We share not only our sorrow but also our coping strategies, our hopes for the future, and our commitment to keeping our children's memories alive.

One way I've honored DJ is by supporting organizations dedicated to suicide prevention. Whether through raising funds, volunteering, or spreading the word about available resources, I've found that even small actions can have a significant impact. I've participated in fundraising walks, organized community events, and collaborated with mental health professionals to create awareness campaigns. These efforts are my way of ensuring DJ's light continues to shine, helping others find hope and support in their darkest moments. Each dollar raised and each conversation sparked feels like a tribute to him—a way to channel my grief into something constructive and meaningful.

Another important part of honoring his legacy has been finding moments of joy and gratitude amid grief. For me, this means celebrating his life rather than focusing solely on his loss. On his birthday, we gather as a family to remember him; to share stories, laugh, and cry. We release balloons in his honor, each carrying a message of love and remembrance. These rituals help us feel connected to him, even though he's no longer with us. I've also started planting a tree in his memory, a living tribute that will grow and provide shade, just as his love continues to nurture us.

DJ's legacy is one of love, kindness, and resilience. It lives on in the lives he touched, the people he helped, and the family that continues to honor him. While his physical presence is gone, his spirit remains a guiding force, pushing us to bring light and hope to others, just as he did.

Honoring his legacy is not only about preserving the past,—it is about actively engaging in the present and shaping a future where love, compassion, and understanding triumph over despair. In this way, DJ's legacy lives on, not only in my heart but in the hearts of all who choose to carry forward the message of hope he embodied.

Through honoring his memory, I find purpose in my pain. Each act of remembrance, each story shared, and each moment of advocacy is a step toward healing—not just for myself, but for others as well. In this journey, I've discovered that while loss can feel insurmountable, love can transform grief into a legacy of hope that uplifts and inspires countless others.

I am committed to ensuring that DJ's light continues to shine, guiding the path for those struggling in darkness, just as he would have wanted.

CHAPTER 6
Through His Son's Eyes

One of the most bittersweet aspects of this journey has been watching my grandson, Terrion, who was just two years old when his father, DJ, passed away. Even at such a young age, he carries the essence of his father within him. He has DJ's smile—bright, warm, and full of life—a smile that lights up any room just as his father's once did. His laughter, too, is a melody that echoes with joy, reminiscent of the way DJ's laughter could fill our hearts with warmth. It's a beautiful yet painful reminder that even though DJ is no longer with us, a part of him lives on in his son, filling our lives with echoes of his love.

There are days when I see my grandson acting just like his father. Whether it's the way he dances, sings, or plays with his toys, it's as if DJ's spirit is shining through him. One unforgettable moment was when he ran into the room wearing his father's old T-shirt, dragging a toy guitar behind him. He grinned up at me and said, "Look, Nana! I'm like Daddy!" That moment brought me to tears—a mixture of joy at seeing DJ in him and sorrow at knowing DJ wasn't there to witness it himself. In that moment, I felt an overwhelming mix of pride and heartbreak: pride in the beautiful boy Terrion is becoming, and heartbreak in the absence of the man who should have been there to guide him.

One memory that stands out is the day after DJ passed. Terrion was playing outside when he suddenly became surrounded by a flurry of white butterflies. He looked up at me with wide eyes and said, "Nana, that's my daddy making sure I'm okay." His innocent belief was both heartwarming and heartbreaking. I could see the purity of his heart as he tried to make sense of the world around him. Sometimes, when he notices the hurt in my face or the tears in my eyes, he asks, "Nana, are you crying because you miss Daddy?" I reply softly, "Yes, baby." In those moments, he reassures me, saying, "My daddy told me to tell you that he loves you and that he got his wings, so Daddy is okay, Nana." Moments like this, filled with his tender understanding and connection to his father, are ones I cherish deeply.

The way Terrion smiles at me, just like DJ did, brings both joy and pain. It's joyful because it reminds me of the incredible love DJ shared with the world, but painful because I know DJ isn't here to see it firsthand. His son is growing up without the man who was once his whole world. At such a young age, my grandson has experienced a loss most people cannot imagine.

Explaining his father's death to him has been one of the hardest things I've ever had to do. I try my best to tell him stories about DJ, to remind him of the love his father had for him. Finding the right words to explain something so final to a child who still sees the world through innocent eyes is a challenge I never imagined facing. There are moments when Terrion asks, "Where is Daddy?" or "When will Daddy come back?" and it breaks my heart. How do you explain something so permanent to a child who doesn't yet fully understand the world?

I tell him that Daddy is in heaven now, watching over him, and that he will always be with us in our hearts. I remind him of the times he and his father shared: how DJ used to sing to him, how they would laugh and play. I hold onto the hope that these memories provide him comfort and a sense of connection to the father who loved him so deeply.

I've made it my mission to ensure that my grandson knows who his father was. I tell him stories about how DJ would make people laugh, how much he loved life, and how deeply he cared for his family. Keeping DJ's memory alive through stories, pictures, and traditions helps bridge the gap left by his absence. One day, I showed him pictures of DJ as a little boy, and his face lit up. "That's me!" he exclaimed, pointing at his father's childhood photo. I laughed and said, "No, baby, that's Daddy when he was your age. But you do look just like him."

In those moments, I see the spark of recognition in Terrion's eyes, as if he is beginning to understand that they are connected in ways that go beyond time and space. I want him to know that DJ was not just a father; he was a person full of dreams, laughter, and creativity. I share stories of the songs DJ wrote, the dreams he pursued, and the love he poured into everything he did. I want Terrion to know that he comes from a lineage of passion and talent, and that his father's spirit lives on in every note of music he hears and every song he sings.

There are days when I wonder how my grandson will grow up, and I wish with all my heart that DJ were here to see it. I imagine the lessons DJ would have taught him: the songs they would have sung together, the games they would have played, and the values DJ would have passed down. I picture them exploring the world together, DJ guiding him through life's ups and downs, sharing moments of laughter and joy. Even in his absence, I find solace in knowing that DJ's influence will shape Terrion through the stories we share and the principles we instill.

Sometimes, when I watch Terrion play, I see him doing things that remind me of DJ: his natural rhythm as he dances to music, his infectious laughter filling the room, and his creativity in building with blocks or drawing pictures. It's as if DJ's essence lives on in Terrion. I often find myself smiling through tears, feeling a bittersweet mix of pride and longing. Through his eyes, I see both the weight of loss and the enduring power of love. His laughter, his smile, and his boundless energy remind me that DJ's love is a force that transcends time and space. While DJ may no longer be physically present, his legacy lives on in his son, showing that love truly endures beyond even the deepest loss. I hold onto the belief that DJ is watching over us, proud of the young boy Terrion is becoming, and that in each moment of joy, he is still with us in spirit.

As I nurture Terrion's connection to his father, I also recognize the importance of allowing him to express his feelings about the loss. There are moments when he grows quiet, and I encourage him to talk about his dad, to share his thoughts and emotions. I want him to know that it's okay to feel sad, to miss his father, and to carry that love with him. I remind him that grief reflects the depth of the love we share and is a journey we can navigate together.

We often look at the stars at night, and I tell him that each one is a reminder of the love that surrounds us: even when we can't see it, it's always there. I point out the brightest star and say, "That's Daddy's star, shining down on you." In these moments, I see the comfort it brings him and hope he understands that while his father may not be here in body, his spirit will always be a guiding light in his life.

Ultimately, I realize that as much as I want to honor DJ's memory, it is equally important to celebrate the life Terrion is living. I strive to create a nurturing environment filled with love, laughter, and creativity, just as DJ would have wanted. I want Terrion to know that he carries his father's legacy within him and that his life is a continuation of that love.

As we move forward together, I am filled with hope for the future. I know that DJ's spirit will always be a part of our family, and through Terrion, his legacy will continue to shine brightly. I want my grandson to grow up understanding who his father was and the profound impact he had on our lives. As he navigates life's challenges, I hope he carries with him the love and lessons of his father. A love that is timeless and a legacy that endures.

This journey of remembrance and healing is not just about looking back; it is also about embracing the present and nurturing the future. I want Terrion to grow up knowing that he is surrounded by love, that he is never alone, and that his father's spirit will always be a part of him. Together, we will create new memories, celebrate milestones, and honor DJ's legacy in every step we take. In doing so, we will ensure that the love DJ had for his family continues to flourish, lighting the way for generations to come.

CHAPTER 7

Spreading Awareness and Prevention
The Power of Breaking the Silence

If there's one thing my son DJ's story has taught me, it's that mental health struggles often remain hidden beneath the surface. Even those who seem happy and full of life, those who are always there for others can be quietly fighting battles we know nothing about. That's why awareness and prevention are critical.

We can't bring DJ back, but we can create a world where more people feel safe sharing their struggles and seeking help. The first step in prevention is breaking the silence around mental health and suicide. For too long, these topics have been treated as taboo—avoided because they make us uncomfortable. But silence only deepens the stigma, making it harder for those who are struggling to reach out.

One of the most heartbreaking realizations I've had during this journey is how many people hesitate to ask for help because they don't want to seem weak. This harmful belief that seeking support is a sign of failure has kept far too many people from getting the help they need. For DJ, and for so many others like him, strength was something he felt he had to project at all times. He was the one people turned to for support—the one who brought joy and laughter into their lives. To admit he was struggling would have felt, in his mind, like letting people down. But the truth is, asking for help isn't a sign of weakness; it is an act of courage.

Recognizing Silent Struggles

Another critical aspect of prevention is recognizing the warning signs that someone may be struggling with suicidal thoughts. These signs aren't always obvious, and many people go out of their way to hide their pain. But there are subtle cues we can watch for:

Changes in Behavior: Withdrawing from loved ones, losing interest in hobbies, or neglecting responsibilities.

Verbal Cues: Comments like, "The world would be better off without me," or even joking about death.

Emotional Shifts: Sudden calmness after a period of distress, or drastic mood swings.

Physical Signs: Changes in eating or sleeping habits or appearing constantly fatigued.

If you notice any of these signs, don't hesitate to reach out. Sometimes, a simple "Are you okay?" can open the door to a life-saving conversation.

Practical Ways to Support Others

Supporting someone who is struggling with mental health isn't always easy, but it's one of the most powerful things you can do. Here are a few ways to help:

Listen Without Judgment: Let them share their thoughts and feelings without interruption. Avoid offering immediate solutions; instead, let them know their emotions are valid.

Encourage Professional Help: Suggest they talk to a therapist, counselor, or trusted medical professional. Offer to help them find resources or even accompany them to their first appointment.

Stay Present: Check in regularly, whether it's through a quick text, a phone call, or spending time together. Consistent support can make all the difference.

Educate Yourself: Learn about mental health conditions and suicide prevention so you can better understand what they're going through.

A Call to Action

If you're reading this and you're struggling, please know this: you are not alone. There is help, and there is hope. Reach out to a trusted friend, family member, or professional. Call a hotline. Send a text. Your life matters, and there are people who care about you more than you realize.

Advocacy and Education

Raising awareness about mental health is a responsibility we all share. Advocacy and education are powerful tools for breaking the cycle of silence and stigma surrounding mental health and suicide. When we advocate for change and educate ourselves and others, we create a society where seeking help is not a sign of weakness but a courageous and necessary step toward healing. For me, writing this book is one way to contribute to that mission. Sharing DJ's story is not easy, but I believe it is necessary. His life, his struggles, and his legacy serve as a reminder that no one is immune to mental health challenges—and no one has to face them alone.

Advocacy doesn't have to rely on big gestures; small actions can create real impact. Sharing helpful resources online, joining community events like the Out of the Darkness Walk, or starting a simple conversation with friends or family all matter. Every effort counts. Advocacy is about speaking up for people who feel unseen, reminding others that it's okay to struggle, and helping build a culture rooted in understanding and support.

The Power of Education

Education is just as critical. Understanding the signs of mental health struggles, the factors that contribute to suicidal thoughts, and the resources available can save lives. Organizations like the American Foundation for Suicide Prevention (AFSP) provide invaluable support, from crisis hotlines to educational programs. I encourage readers to get involved—whether by volunteering, donating, or spreading the word about these essential tools.

By advocating for change and educating ourselves, we can move toward a world where mental health is treated with the same importance as physical health. Together, we can create a society in which everyone feels supported, valued, and seen.

CHAPTER 8

The Impact of Suicide on Our Community

Suicide is a word that carries immense weight, evoking fear, sadness, and confusion. It is a reality that profoundly affects our communities, especially the younger generation, yet it remains shrouded in silence and stigma. In a world where mental health struggles often go unseen, we face a painful truth: we know suicide occurs, but we rarely talk about it. This silence is not just uncomfortable, it is dangerous.

Since beginning my journey of grief and healing after losing my son, DJ, I have met countless individuals wrestling with loss. People who have lost loved ones to suicide or mental illness. Each story is a stark reminder that behind every statistic lies a human life, a family torn apart, and a community left to pick up the pieces. Witnessing the widespread nature of this tragedy is heartbreaking, yet it is equally frustrating to see how often it is dismissed or ignored.

The reality is that suicide does not discriminate. It does not consider socioeconomic status, education, or outward appearances. We often fall into the trap of believing mental illness shows only in those who are visibly struggling—those who seem sad, withdrawn, or troubled. This assumption could not be further from the truth. Mental illness wears many faces; it can hide behind a smile, a polished appearance, or a life that seems outwardly successful. Just because someone appears "okay" does not mean they are not fighting a battle within.

Through conversations with bereaved families and individuals who have faced their own struggles, I have come to understand the wisdom in the saying, "Never judge a book by its cover." We cannot rely solely on outward appearances to gauge a person's emotional state. Mental illness can be silent, insidious, and often masked by the pressures of daily life. People often feel compelled to put on a brave face, projecting strength and stability while suffering in silence. This is where the tragedy lies: individuals who are hurting, who need help, but feel they cannot reach out for fear of being misunderstood or judged.

As a community, we must do better. We need to cultivate an environment where open dialogue about mental health and suicide is not only accepted but encouraged. It is time to challenge the stigma surrounding these topics. We must move beyond polite small talk and ask the questions that matter. Instead of merely asking, "Are you okay?" we must ask, "Are you really okay?" This small shift in language can open the door to deeper conversations, allowing individuals to share their true feelings and struggles without fear of judgment.

In my experience, genuinely asking someone how they are doing can have a profound impact. It can be the lifeline someone desperately needs. But we must also be prepared to listen without judgment and to offer support unconditionally. We should create safe spaces where people feel comfortable sharing their stories, where vulnerability is met with empathy rather than stigma. We need to acknowledge that everyone has their battles, and sometimes the strongest among us are those silently suffering the most.

As a society, we must recognize that mental health is just as important as physical health. We need to advocate for mental health education in schools, workplaces, and communities, ensuring that everyone has access to resources and support. We must challenge the narrative that mental illness is a personal failing or a sign of weakness. Instead, we should promote understanding and compassion, emphasizing that seeking help is a sign of strength.

It is also vital to recognize that young people today face unique challenges that can exacerbate mental health issues. Social media, academic pressures, and uncertainty about the future can weigh heavily on their shoulders. We must remain attuned to these pressures and create environments where young people feel safe expressing their feelings and seeking help. By breaking the silence surrounding suicide and mental health, we can help dismantle the barriers that prevent individuals from reaching out for support.

I have learned that sharing stories of loss and resilience can be a powerful tool for healing. When we open up about our experiences, we not only honor our loved ones but also invite others to share their own stories. These conversations can spark change, inspire action, and foster a sense of community and understanding. We must be willing to confront uncomfortable truths about mental health and suicide, because it is only through awareness and compassion that we can begin to heal.

In conclusion, we must commit to breaking the silence surrounding suicide and mental health issues. We owe it to those we have lost, to those still struggling, and to future generations. Let us create a society where mental health is prioritized, where individuals are truly seen and heard, and where no one has to suffer in silence. Together, we can cultivate a culture of understanding, compassion, and hope—a culture that empowers individuals to seek help and reminds us that we are never truly alone.

It's time to talk, to share, and to support one another. When we break the silence, we break the cycle of despair. In doing so, we honor the memories of those we have lost and pave the way for a brighter, more compassionate future. We must embrace uncomfortable conversations, challenge the stigma, and create a community where vulnerability is met with understanding. By fostering an environment of openness, we can encourage those who are struggling to reach out, share their burdens, and seek the help they need.

Let us remember that every life lost to suicide is a reminder of the importance of connection and support. Each story of struggle is an opportunity to learn, grow, and become advocates for change. We can be the voices that speak for those who feel unheard, the hands that reach out to those in need, and the hearts that embrace the pain of others with compassion.

As we move forward, let us commit to a proactive approach to mental health. This means educating ourselves and advocating for policies that support mental health initiatives, ensuring resources reach those who need them most. It means standing together as a community, united in our mission to break the silence and foster a culture of acceptance and understanding.

In sharing this chapter, I hope to inspire others to join this vital conversation. Together, we can create a ripple effect of awareness and compassion that reaches far beyond our immediate circles. Let us honor the lives of those we have lost by ensuring their stories are not forgotten but instead serve as catalysts for change.

Ultimately, it is our collective responsibility to ensure that no one feels alone in their struggles. By breaking the silence, we not only honor the memories of those we have lost but also create a legacy of hope for future generations. Let us be the change we wish to see, fostering a community where mental health is prioritized and every individual feels valued and supported.

CHAPTER 9

A Legacy of Hope and Love
Honoring His Life

When I first began writing this book, I was unsure how I would find the strength to turn my pain into words. Reliving the moments of loss, grief, and heartbreak felt like wading through a sea of sorrow, one that threatened to overwhelm me. Each keystroke reminded me of the void left by my son, DJ. Yet, as I poured my heart onto the pages, I came to a profound realization: this book isn't merely about my anguish. It is a celebration of DJ's life, his radiant light, and the love he freely shared with everyone fortunate enough to know him. It is about his legacy—a legacy I hope will inspire hope and understanding in others.

DJ was far more than the way he left this world. He was a loving father, a devoted son, a caring grandson, and a true friend to many. His laughter could brighten even the darkest days, and his heart was large enough to embrace everyone around him. Sharing his story is not just a way to remember him. It is my promise to ensure his love and kindness endure.

Every year, my family and I participate in the Out of the Darkness Walk to honor DJ's memory and raise awareness about suicide prevention. Walking alongside others who have experienced similar losses reminds me that we are not alone in our grief. Together, we share stories, laughter, and even tears, forming connections that strengthen and sustain us. In those moments, the weight of sorrow is eased by the understanding that we are part of a larger community, united in our care for those we have lost.

Carrying His Light Forward

Through my grandson, DJ's spirit continues to shine. His smile, laughter, and curiosity are daily reminders of the love DJ brought into the world. Watching my grandson grow is both comforting and challenging. I see so much of DJ in him—the same twinkle in his eyes, the same boundless energy. While this brings immense joy, it also deepens the ache of knowing DJ isn't here to witness these moments.

Yet, I find solace in knowing DJ's legacy lives on in his son. It is a reminder that love endures beyond loss and that the impact of a well-lived life extends far beyond the years we are given. My grandson carries forward DJ's essence and, in some ways, allows me to relive the moments I cherished with him. Together, we create new memories, bridging past and present, ensuring that DJ is never truly gone.

Turning Pain into Purpose

One of the greatest lessons I've learned on this journey is that healing doesn't mean forgetting. It means finding purpose amidst the pain. By sharing my story, advocating for mental health awareness, and supporting others who are struggling, I have found a way to honor DJ's life and ensure his story makes a difference.

I have spoken at events, revealing the raw truth of our experiences and encouraging others to break the silence around mental health. It hasn't always been easy; some days, the weight of grief feels insurmountable. But with each story I share, a flicker of hope ignites within me. Each time someone tells me that DJ's story helped them or gave them the courage to seek help, I am reminded of my purpose. A purpose that transcends my pain and transforms it into something meaningful.

DJ's presence is deeply woven into my life. With every step I take to raise awareness and every tear that falls in his memory, I feel his light guiding me. Through this journey, I have learned that while the pain of losing him will never fully fade, the love we shared continues to shape the path ahead. As I carry his legacy forward, I hold onto the hope that we can create a world where conversations about mental health are open, and where love overcomes despair.

CHAPTER 10

A Message for You
To Those Grieving

To anyone grieving, know that you are not alone. Grief can feel like an overwhelming burden, wrapping around your shoulders and isolating you. It whispers lies, suggesting you should bear this pain in silence or that your sorrow is too much for others. I urge you to reject that notion. Lean on your loved ones; allow them to support you, to hold you when the weight feels too heavy.

Reach out for help, even when it seems impossible. Give yourself the grace to heal at your own pace—there is no right or wrong way to grieve. Your journey is uniquely yours, shaped by love, loss, and the memories you carry. There will be days when the pain is sharp and relentless and others when moments of joy appear alongside sorrow. Accept each feeling as it comes. Allow yourself to cry, to laugh, and to remember. Every aspect of grief has its place.

To Those Struggling

To those struggling with their mental health, I want you to know this: your life is precious, and you are loved more than you can imagine. Even during the darkest hours, when it feels as though the weight of the world is pressing down on you, there is hope.

Help is available, and it is within reach. Please don't hesitate to reach out to a friend, a family member, or a professional who can guide you through the shadows. Your story isn't over. There are people who want to walk this journey with you, who want to hear your voice, understand your pain, and remind you that you matter.

I know firsthand the depths of despair that can cloud your vision, making it difficult to see even a glimmer of light. But that light exists, waiting for you to grasp it, to let it fill the empty spaces within. You are not a burden; you are a beautiful soul who deserves to find peace and joy again.

To Everyone Else

And to everyone else, I ask you to be a light in someone else's life. Your kindness can pierce through even the darkest moments. Check in on your loved ones, have the difficult conversations that might feel uncomfortable, and let people know they are cared for. Every act of kindness, no matter how small, can create ripples of hope.

Let's work together to create a world where no one feels alone in their struggles. A world where understanding and compassion prevail. Your willingness to listen, to reach out, and to extend a hand can make a meaningful difference in someone's journey.

Hope for the Future

While I will always carry the pain of losing DJ, I also carry his love, his laughter, and his light. His story does not end with his passing; it lives on in the hearts of those he touched, in the family and friends who continue to honor him, and in the work we do to spread awareness and save lives. Each day, I strive to turn my sorrow into action, transforming my grief into a beacon of hope for others navigating their own darkness.

On some days, when I see a butterfly flutter by or hear a song that reminds me of DJ, I feel his presence so strongly. It is as if he is reaching out to remind me that love transcends even the deepest pain and that our souls remain connected despite physical distance. Writing this book has been a journey of healing, purpose, and carrying DJ's light forward.

My hope is that his story, and my own, will continue to shine in the lives of others, reminding us all that even in the darkest moments, there is always hope. You are not defined by your pain but by the love you continue to share and the light you choose to carry.

To my son, DJ, I will always carry you in my heart. Your light will never fade, and your legacy will never be forgotten. You are my reason to keep going, my reason to keep sharing, and my reason to believe in a brighter future. Every word I write is a tribute to you—a promise that your story will inspire others to seek help and find hope.

As I navigate this journey of healing, I hold onto the belief that together we can create a world where love conquers despair and where every individual feels valued and understood. Your spirit guides me, DJ, and I will continue to honor you by spreading the message that life, with all its struggles, is a gift worth cherishing.

CHAPTER 11

The Impact of Suicide on Our Community

Suicide is a word that carries a heavy weight, a word that can send shivers down the spine and evoke feelings of fear, sadness, and confusion. It is a reality that affects our community, especially the younger generation, yet it is a topic that remains shrouded in silence and stigma. In a world where mental health struggles are often invisible, we find ourselves grappling with a profound truth: we know suicide happens, but we rarely talk about it. This silence is not just uncomfortable; it is dangerous.

Since embarking on this journey of grief and healing, I have encountered countless individuals grappling with loss: people who have lost loved ones to suicide or mental illness. Each story I hear serves as a poignant reminder that behind every statistic is a human life, a family torn apart, and a community left to pick up the pieces. It is heartbreaking to witness how widespread this tragedy is, yet it is equally frustrating to see how often it is dismissed or ignored.

The truth is that suicide does not discriminate. It does not care about socioeconomic status, education level, or outward appearances. We often fall into the trap of believing that mental illness looks a certain way, that it manifests only in those who are visibly struggling, those who appear sad or withdrawn. This stereotype could not be further from the truth. Mental illness can wear many faces; it can hide behind a smile, a well-kept appearance, or a life filled with apparent success. Just because someone seems "okay" on the outside does not mean they are not fighting a battle within.

In my conversations with bereaved families and individuals who have faced their own struggles, I have come to realize the profound wisdom in the saying, "Never judge a book by its cover." We cannot rely solely on outward appearances to gauge a person's emotional state. It is essential to understand that mental illness can be silent, insidious, and often masked by the pressures of daily life. People may feel compelled to put on a brave face, to project an image of strength and stability, all while suffering in silence. This is where the tragedy lies: people who are hurting, who need help, but who feel they cannot reach out because they fear being misunderstood or judged.

As a community, we must do better. We need to cultivate an environment where open dialogue about mental health and suicide is not only accepted but encouraged. It is time to challenge the stigma that surrounds these topics. We need to move beyond the polite small talk and ask the questions that matter. Instead of merely asking, "Are you okay?" we must learn to ask, "Are you really okay?" This simple shift in language can open the door to deeper conversations, allowing individuals to share their true feelings and struggles without fear of judgment.

In my experience, the act of asking how someone is doing can have a profound impact. It can be the lifeline that someone desperately needs. But we must also be prepared to listen without judgment and offer support without conditions. We should create safe spaces where people feel comfortable sharing their stories, where vulnerability is met with empathy rather than stigma. We need to acknowledge that everyone has their battles, and sometimes, the strongest among us are those who are silently suffering the most.

As a society, we must recognize that mental health is just as important as physical health. We need to advocate for mental health education in schools, workplaces, and communities, ensuring that everyone has access to resources and support. We must challenge the narrative that mental illness is a personal failing or a sign of weakness. Instead, we should promote understanding and compassion, emphasizing that seeking help is a sign of strength.

It is also vital to acknowledge that young people today face unique challenges that can exacerbate mental health issues. Social media, academic pressures, and the uncertainty of the future can weigh heavily on their shoulders. We must be attuned to these pressures and create an environment where young people feel safe to express their feelings and seek help. By breaking the silence surrounding suicide and mental health, we can help dismantle the barriers that prevent individuals from reaching out for support.

I have learned that sharing stories of loss and resilience can be a powerful tool for healing. When we open up about our experiences, we not only honor our loved ones but also invite others to share their own stories. These conversations can spark change, inspire action, and foster a sense of community and understanding. We must be willing to confront the uncomfortable truths about mental health and suicide, for it is only through awareness and compassion that we can begin to heal.

In conclusion, we must commit ourselves to breaking the silence surrounding suicide and mental health issues. We owe it to those we have lost, to those who are still struggling, and to future generations. Let us create a society where mental health is prioritized, where individuals are seen and heard, and where no one has to suffer in silence. Together, we can cultivate a culture of understanding, compassion, and hope: a culture that empowers individuals to seek help and reminds us all that we are never alone.

It's time to talk, to share, and to support one another. Because when we break the silence, we break the cycle of despair. And in doing so, we honor the memories of those we have lost while paving the way for a brighter, more compassionate future.

EPILOGUE

As I complete this book, I find myself reflecting not only on the loss of my son but also on the remarkable ways his life continues to touch others. What began as an effort to process my grief has grown into a mission: to inspire change, encourage conversations about mental health, and remind others that they are never alone.

The journey has not been easy. Reliving the memories, the pain, and the unanswered questions has been one of the hardest things I have ever done. Yet it has also been healing. It has allowed me to see DJ's life in its entirety— not just how it ended, but how he lived: with love, laughter, and an indomitable spirit that still shines.

I hope this book serves as a source of comfort, connection, and action. To those who are grieving, may it remind you that healing is possible. To those struggling, may it show you that your life matters. And to everyone else, may it inspire you to reach out, listen, and be a light in someone else's life.

DJ's story does not end here. It continues through his son, his family, the lives he touched, and the hearts that carry his memory forward. It also lives on in you, dear reader, as you carry this message into the world. Thank you for walking this journey with me. Together, we can make a difference.

ABOUT THE AUTHOR

Tonya Jones was born and raised in Sterlington, Louisiana, and currently resides in Cedar Hill, Texas. She served as a Hospital Corpsman in the United States Navy and has over 15 years of experience as a nurse, specializing in various areas of healthcare. Her career in nursing was fueled by an unwavering desire to help others, a passion that has defined much of her life. However, it is her role as a mother that has had the most profound impact on her journey. The tragic loss of her son, DJ, transformed her in ways she never could have anticipated.

As a medical professional, she spent years saving lives, yet she was unable to save the one that mattered most: her own child. The weight of that loss, coupled with the guilt and pain, became an unimaginable burden, one that she hopes no other parent will ever have to endure. Through this book, Tonya seeks to honor DJ's memory and bring awareness to the silent struggles of mental health. She hopes that by sharing her story, others will feel encouraged to speak up, seek help, and understand that mental health challenges should never be faced alone. Her journey of grief and healing has deepened her passion for suicide prevention and mental health advocacy, leading her to support other families navigating the complexities of loss and healing.

Tonya continues to channel her pain into purpose, advocating for mental health awareness and encouraging open conversations about the realities of grief. She carries DJ's light with her in everything she does, ensuring that his love, his story, and his legacy live on. She lives with her family, cherishing every moment, and using her voice to bring hope and healing to others who need it most.

BREAKING THE SILENCE

TONYA JONES

www.ingramcontent.com/pod-product-compliance
Lightning Source LLC
Chambersburg PA
CBHW051229120626
46547CB00013B/1566